Better Homes and Gardens.

Vegetarian

Easy Everyday Recipe Library

BETTER HOMES AND GARDENS® BOOKS

Des Moines, Iowa

EASY EVERYDAY RECIPE LIBRARY

Better Homes and Gardens® Books, An imprint of Meredith® Books
Published for Creative World Enterprises LP, West Chester, Pennsylvania
www.creativeworldcooking.com

Vegetarian
Project Editors: Spectrum Communication Services, Inc.
Project Designers: Seif Visual Communications
Copy Chief: Catherine Hamrick
Copy and Production Editor: Terri Fredrickson
Contributing Proofreaders: Kathy Eastman, Susan J. Kling
Electronic Production Coordinator: Paula Forest
Editorial and Design Assistants: Judy Bailey, Mary Lee Gavin, Karen Schirm
Test Kitchen Director: Lynn Blanchard
Production Director: Douglas M. Johnston
Production Managers: Pam Kvitne, Marjorie J. Schenkelberg

Meredith® Books
Editor in Chief: James D. Blume
Design Director: Matt Strelecki
Managing Editor: Gregory H. Kayko

Director, Sales & Marketing, Retail: Michael A. Peterson
Director, Sales & Marketing, Special Markets: Rita McMullen
Director, Sales & Marketing, Home & Garden Center Channel: Ray Wolf
Director, Operations: George A. Susral

Vice President, General Manager: Jamie L. Martin

Better Homes and Gardens® Magazine
Editor in Chief: Jean LemMon
Executive Food Editor: Nancy Byal

Meredith Publishing Group
President, Publishing Group: Christopher M. Little
Vice President, Consumer Marketing & Development: Hal Oringer

Meredith Corporation
Chairman and Chief Executive Officer: William T. Kerr

Chairman of the Executive Committee: E. T. Meredith III

Creative World Enterprises LP
Publisher: Richard J. Petrone
Design Consultants to Creative World Enterprises: Coastline Studios, Orlando, Florida

All of us at Better Homes and Gardens® Books are dedicated to providing you with the information and ideas you need to create delicious foods. We welcome your comments and suggestions. Write to us at: Better Homes and Gardens Books, Cookbook Editorial Department, 1716 Locust St., Des Moines, Iowa 50309-3023.

Our seal assures you that every recipe in *Vegetarian* has been tested in the Better Homes and Gardens® Test Kitchen. This means that each recipe is practical and reliable, and meets our high standards of taste appeal. We guarantee your satisfaction with this book for as long as you own it.

Cover photo: Grilled Vegetable Salad with Garlic Dressing (see recipe, page 42)

Planning meals around foods other than meat frees us to explore all kinds of new dishes. Beans, lentils, eggs, cheeses, pasta, and rice are the beginnings of many great-tasting recipes that are sure to become your family's favorites.

If you think you'll have trouble convincing family members that meatless meals are worth trying, serve them Spicy Black Bean Chili. This zesty concoction is so full of beans, they'll never miss the meat. Or try Cheesy Vegetable Lasagna, a twist on a classic brightened with broccoli and carrots.

Give meat-free dining a try—you'll discover a wealth of healthful foods that taste as good as they look.

CONTENTS

Spicy Black Beans and Rice

Instead of rice, spoon the warm black bean mixture over squares of freshly baked corn bread.

1 medium onion, chopped (½ cup)
4 cloves garlic, minced
2 tablespoons olive oil or cooking oil
1 15-ounce can black beans, rinsed and drained
1 14½-ounce can Mexican-style stewed tomatoes
⅛ to ¼ teaspoon ground red pepper
2 cups hot cooked brown or long grain rice
¼ cup chopped onion (optional)

In a medium saucepan cook ½ cup onion and garlic in hot oil till tender. Carefully stir in the drained beans, undrained tomatoes, and red pepper. Bring to boiling; reduce heat. Simmer, uncovered, for 15 minutes.

To serve, mound rice on dinner plates; make a well in the centers. Spoon black bean mixture into centers. If desired, sprinkle with ¼ cup onion. Makes 4 servings.

Nutrition information per serving: 279 calories, 11 g protein, 47 g carbohydrate, 8 g fat (1 g saturated), 0 mg cholesterol, 631 mg sodium.

Warm Beans with Herbed Tomatoes And Goat Cheese

Get extra mileage out of this recipe by chilling any leftovers and serving them as salad with warm tortillas.

3 medium ripe tomatoes, seeded and chopped (2 cups)
¼ cup snipped fresh basil
¼ cup snipped fresh oregano
2 green onions, sliced
1 clove garlic, minced
½ teaspoon salt
¼ teaspoon pepper
1 15-ounce can small red beans or kidney beans
1 15-ounce can great northern beans or navy beans
4 ounces semisoft goat (chèvre) cheese or feta cheese, crumbled (1 cup)

In a medium bowl combine tomatoes, basil, oregano, green onions, garlic, salt, and pepper. Let stand at room temperature for 30 minutes to 2 hours.

In a medium saucepan combine undrained red or kidney beans and undrained great northern or navy beans. Bring to boiling; reduce heat. Cover and simmer about 2 minutes or till heated through. Drain.

To serve, toss warm beans with tomato mixture. Sprinkle with cheese. Serve warm. Makes 4 servings.

Nutrition information per serving: 304 calories, 22 g protein, 45 g carbohydrate, 7 g fat (4 g saturated), 13 mg cholesterol, 558 mg sodium.

Spicy Black Beans and Rice

Hearty Rice Skillet

Another time, vary the taste by using a can of flavored stewed tomatoes—Mexican, Cajun, or Italian.

1   15-ounce can black, garbanzo, or
      kidney beans, rinsed and drained
1   14½-ounce can stewed tomatoes,
      cut up
2   cups loose-pack frozen mixed
      vegetables
1   cup water
¾   cup quick-cooking brown rice
½   teaspoon dried thyme, crushed, or
      dillweed
      Several dashes bottled hot pepper
      sauce (optional)
1   10¾-ounce can condensed tomato
      soup
⅓   cup slivered almonds, toasted
½   cup shredded mozzarella or cheddar
      cheese (2 ounces)

In a large skillet stir together the beans, undrained stewed tomatoes, frozen vegetables, water, uncooked rice, thyme or dillweed, and, if desired, hot pepper sauce. Bring to boiling; reduce heat. Cover and simmer for 12 to 14 minutes or till rice is tender. Stir in tomato soup; heat through.

Before serving, stir in almonds. Sprinkle with cheese. Makes 4 servings.

Nutrition information per serving: 354 calories, 19 g protein, 57 g carbohydrate, 10 g fat (2 g saturated), 8 mg cholesterol, 1,244 mg sodium.

Couscous Tacos

Couscous (KOOS-koos) is a quick-cooking grain made from ground semolina in the shape of very tiny beads. Look for it in the rice or pasta section of your supermarket or at specialty stores.

1   14½-ounce can Mexican-style
       stewed tomatoes
1   cup water
¼   cup chopped onion
½   of a 1⅛- or 1¼-ounce envelope
       (5 teaspoons) taco seasoning mix
⅔   cup couscous
8   ounces firm or extra-firm tofu
       (fresh bean curd), drained and
       finely chopped
10   taco shells, warmed
1½   cups shredded lettuce
⅔   cup shredded cheddar cheese
       Salsa

In a medium saucepan combine undrained stewed tomatoes, water, onion, and taco seasoning mix. Bring to boiling. Stir in couscous and tofu. Cover and remove from heat. Let stand for 5 minutes.

Spoon couscous mixture into taco shells. Top with lettuce and cheese. Serve with salsa. Makes 5 servings.

Nutrition information per serving: 365 calories, 18 g protein, 45 g carbohydrate, 15 g fat (4 g saturated), 16 mg cholesterol, 809 mg sodium.

Cheese Tortellini with Cannellini Bean Sauce

You can make this low-fat pasta dish in a snap thanks to refrigerated tortellini and canned beans. Try it for a busy week night dinner.

1 9-ounce package refrigerated cheese-stuffed tortellini
1 15-ounce can white kidney (cannellini) beans, rinsed and drained
⅔ cup milk
⅔ cup thin slivers of red, yellow, and/or green sweet pepper
¼ cup grated Parmesan cheese
1 tablespoon snipped fresh oregano or 1 teaspoon dried oregano, crushed
¼ teaspoon salt
¼ teaspoon ground nutmeg
⅛ teaspoon black pepper
Finely shredded Parmesan cheese (optional)
Fresh oregano sprigs (optional)

Cook the pasta according to package directions. Drain; keep warm.

Meanwhile, for sauce, in a food processor bowl or blender container combine the beans and milk. Cover and process or blend till smooth. Transfer the bean mixture to a large skillet.

Stir in sweet pepper slivers, grated Parmesan cheese, snipped fresh or dried oregano, salt, nutmeg, and black pepper. Cook and stir till heated through.

Arrange pasta on dinner plates or a large platter. Spoon the sauce over pasta.

If desired, sprinkle each serving with finely shredded Parmesan cheese and garnish with fresh oregano sprigs. Makes 4 servings.

Nutrition information per serving: 304 calories, 21 g protein, 48 g carbohydrate, 6 g fat (2 g saturated), 43 mg cholesterol, 730 mg sodium.

Herbed Pasta Primavera

For the best flavor, use fresh parsley, fresh basil, and freshly shredded Parmesan cheese.

6 ounces packaged dried linguine, spaghetti, or fettuccine
1 cup water
2 teaspoons cornstarch
2 teaspoons instant vegetable or chicken bouillon granules
1 tablespoon olive oil
2 cloves garlic, minced
8 ounces asparagus, cut into 1-inch pieces
2 medium carrots, very thinly bias-sliced
1 medium onion, chopped
1 6-ounce package frozen pea pods, thawed and well drained
⅔ cup sliced almonds or chopped cashews
¼ cup snipped parsley
2 tablespoons snipped fresh basil or 1½ teaspoons dried basil, crushed
¼ teaspoon pepper
⅓ cup finely shredded Parmesan cheese

Cook pasta according to package directions. Drain; keep warm. Meanwhile, for sauce, in a small bowl stir together the water, cornstarch, and vegetable or chicken bouillon granules. Set aside.

Add olive oil to a wok or large skillet. Preheat over medium-high heat. Stir-fry garlic in hot oil for 15 seconds. Add asparagus, carrots, and onion; stir fry for 2 minutes. Add pea pods, nuts, parsley, basil, and pepper. Stir-fry about 1 minute more or till vegetables are crisp-tender. Remove vegetable mixture from wok.

Stir sauce; add to wok. Cook and stir till thickened and bubbly. Cook and stir for 1 minute more. Return vegetable mixture to wok. Cook and stir till heated through. Serve immediately over pasta. Sprinkle with Parmesan cheese. Makes 4 servings.

Nutrition information per serving: 432 calories, 17 g protein, 52 g carbohydrate, 19 g fat (3 g saturated), 7 mg cholesterol, 642 mg sodium.

Gingered Vegetable-Tofu Stir-Fry

Buy extra-firm tofu to prevent it from breaking apart while stir-frying this flavorful dish.

1 cup water
¼ cup dry sherry or dry white wine
2 tablespoons soy sauce
4 teaspoons cornstarch
½ teaspoon sugar
1 tablespoon cooking oil
2 teaspoons grated gingerroot
1 pound asparagus, cut into 1-inch pieces (3 cups), or one 10-ounce package frozen cut asparagus, thawed and well drained
1 small yellow summer squash, halved lengthwise and sliced (1¼ cups)
2 green onions, sliced
1 10½-ounce package extra-firm tofu (fresh bean curd), cut into ½-inch cubes
½ cup pine nuts or chopped almonds, toasted
2 cups hot cooked brown rice

For sauce, in a small bowl stir together water, sherry or wine, soy sauce, cornstarch, and sugar. Set aside.

Add cooking oil to a wok or large skillet. Preheat over medium-high heat (add more oil if necessary during cooking). Stir-fry gingerroot in hot oil for 15 seconds. Add fresh asparagus (if using) and squash; stir-fry for 3 minutes. Add thawed asparagus (if using) and green onions; stir-fry about 1½ minutes more or till asparagus is crisp-tender. Remove from wok.

Add tofu to wok. Gently stir-fry for 2 to 3 minutes or till lightly browned. Remove from wok. Stir sauce; add to wok. Cook and stir till thickened and bubbly.

Return cooked vegetables and tofu to wok. Gently stir all ingredients together to coat. Cover and cook about 1 minute more or till heated through.

Stir in pine nuts or almonds. Serve immediately over hot cooked brown rice. Makes 4 servings.

Nutrition information per serving: 412 calories, 22 g protein, 38 g carbohydrate, 21 g fat (3 g saturated), 0 mg cholesterol, 541 mg sodium.

Tofu Tips

Tofu is soybean curd that's made from soybean milk by a process similar to the one used for making cheese. It's sold in blocks or cakes and comes in soft, firm, and extra-firm styles. Extra-firm tofu is good for stir-fried dishes because it holds its shape well. Look for it in the refrigerated area of your supermarket produce section.

Fresh Vegetable Risotto

Classic risotto is an Italian specialty made by simmering and constantly stirring rice so it slowly absorbs the cooking liquid, resulting in a creamy dish. This one is flavored with colorful vegetables and two cheeses.

2   cups sliced fresh mushrooms
1   medium onion, chopped
2   cloves garlic, minced
2   tablespoons olive oil or cooking oil
1   cup Arborio or long grain rice
3   cups vegetable or chicken broth
¾   cup bite-size asparagus or broccoli
      pieces
1   medium tomato, seeded and
      chopped (⅔ cup)
¼   cup shredded carrot
1   cup shredded fontina or Muenster
      cheese (4 ounces)
¼   cup grated Parmesan cheese
3   tablespoons snipped fresh basil or
      parsley
      Tomato slices (optional)

In a large saucepan cook the mushrooms, onion, and garlic in hot oil till onion is tender. Stir in uncooked rice. Cook and stir for 5 minutes.

Meanwhile, in another saucepan bring the vegetable or chicken broth to boiling; reduce heat and simmer. Slowly add 1 cup of the broth to rice mixture, stirring constantly. Continue to cook and stir over medium heat till liquid is absorbed.

Add another ½ cup of the broth and the asparagus or broccoli to rice mixture, stirring constantly. Continue to cook and stir till the liquid is absorbed. Add another 1 cup broth, ½ cup at a time, stirring constantly till the liquid is absorbed. (This should take about 15 minutes.)

Stir in the chopped tomato, carrot, and the remaining ½ cup broth. Cook and stir till rice is slightly creamy and just tender.

Stir in fontina or Muenster cheese, Parmesan cheese, and basil or parsley. If desired, garnish with tomato slices. Serve immediately. Makes 4 servings.

Nutrition information per serving: 401 calories, 15 g protein, 47 g carbohydrate, 19 g fat (8 g saturated), 38 mg cholesterol, 1,052 mg sodium.

Corn and Green Chili Chowder

During sweet corn season, you can make this chowder using fresh ears of corn. Omit the frozen corn and use a sharp knife to remove the kernels from 2 medium ears of sweet corn.

1 medium onion, chopped
2 tablespoons margarine or butter
2 tablespoons all-purpose flour
2 cups water
1 large potato, peeled and chopped
1 10-ounce package frozen whole
     kernel corn
1 4-ounce can diced green chili
     peppers
1 tablespoon instant vegetable or
     chicken bouillon granules
¼ teaspoon coarsely ground black
     pepper
2 cups milk
2 tablespoons snipped cilantro or
     parsley
   Cilantro or parsley sprigs (optional)
   Sliced fresh chili peppers (optional)

In a large saucepan cook onion in margarine or butter till tender. Stir in flour. Add water, potato, frozen corn, canned green chili peppers, bouillon granules, and black pepper. Bring to boiling; reduce heat. Cover and simmer about 10 minutes or till potato is tender. Stir in the milk and 2 tablespoons cilantro or parsley. Heat through.

To serve, ladle chowder into soup bowls. If desired, garnish each serving with cilantro or parsley sprigs and fresh chili peppers. Makes 4 servings.

Nutrition information per serving: 234 calories, 8 g protein, 34 g carbohydrate, 9 g fat (1 g saturated), 9 mg cholesterol, 944 mg sodium.

Hearty Green Gumbo

The "green" in this Cajun-style soup comes from a mixture of spinach, watercress, and parsley. If you don't have watercress, simply increase the parsley to 2 bunches.

1   10-ounce package frozen chopped spinach
1   bunch watercress, chopped (2 cups)
1   bunch parsley, chopped (2 cups)
¼   cup water
½   cup all-purpose flour
½   cup cooking oil
2   large onions, chopped
2   stalks celery, chopped
1   medium green sweet pepper, chopped
1   teaspoon salt
¼   teaspoon ground red pepper
¼   teaspoon black pepper
1   cup chopped broccoli
1   cup chopped parsnips or rutabaga
1   15-ounce can white kidney (cannellini) beans, rinsed and drained
2   cups hot cooked rice

In a Dutch oven combine spinach, watercress, parsley, and ¼ cup water. Bring to boiling, breaking up spinach with a fork; reduce heat. Cover and simmer for 10 minutes. Drain, reserving cooking liquid. Press out excess liquid from greens with a spatula. Set greens and cooking liquid aside.

For roux, in the same Dutch oven stir together the flour and oil till smooth. Cook over medium-high heat for 5 minutes, stirring constantly. Reduce heat to medium. Cook and stir about 10 minutes more or till roux is light reddish brown. Add onions, celery, and green pepper. Cook and stir for 5 to 10 minutes or till vegetables are very tender.

Add enough water to the reserved cooking liquid to make 2½ cups. Add the liquid, cooked greens, salt, ground red pepper, and black pepper to the onion mixture. Bring to boiling; reduce heat. Cover and simmer for 15 minutes. Stir in broccoli and parsnips or rutabaga. Cover and simmer about 10 minutes more or till tender. Stir in beans; heat through.

To serve, divide rice among soup bowls. Ladle the bean mixture over rice. Makes 6 servings.

Nutrition information per serving: 403 calories, 11 g protein, 53 g carbohydrate, 19 g fat (3 g saturated), 0 mg cholesterol, 548 mg sodium.

Spicy Black Bean Chili

For a complete meal, serve this spicy chili with crusty sourdough bread.

1   cup dry black beans
6   cups cold water
1   medium onion, chopped
4   cloves garlic, minced
1   tablespoon cooking oil
1   tablespoon chili powder
1   teaspoon ground cumin
1   teaspoon dried oregano, crushed
½   teaspoon paprika
¼   teaspoon salt
¼   teaspoon ground red pepper
4   cups vegetable or chicken broth
1   14½-ounce can tomatoes, cut up
¼   cup dry sherry or water
¼   cup plain low-fat yogurt or dairy
      sour cream
    Cilantro sprigs

Rinse beans. In a large saucepan combine the beans and 6 cups water. Bring to boiling; reduce heat. Simmer, uncovered, for 2 minutes. Remove from heat. Cover and let stand for 1 hour. (Or, place beans in water in pan. Cover and soak beans overnight.) Drain and rinse beans.

In a Dutch oven cook the onion and garlic in hot oil till onion is tender. Stir in the chili powder, cumin, oregano, paprika, salt, and ground red pepper. Cook and stir for 1 minute.

Stir in the beans, vegetable or chicken broth, undrained tomatoes, and sherry or water. Bring to boiling; reduce heat. Cover and simmer for 1 to 1½ hours or till the beans are tender.

To serve, ladle the chili into soup bowls. Top each serving with yogurt or sour cream and cilantro sprigs. Makes 4 servings.

Nutrition information per serving: 231 calories, 11 g protein, 38 g carbohydrate, 6 g fat (1 g saturated), 1 mg cholesterol, 1,432 mg sodium.

Split Pea Soup with Spiced Yogurt

Unlike traditional smooth pea soup, this one is full of chunky vegetables and peas and topped with a spicy mixture of seasoned yogurt.

1	cup dry split peas
4	cups vegetable or chicken broth
1	bay leaf
¼	teaspoon dried rosemary, crushed
2	stalks celery, sliced
2	medium carrots, chopped
1	medium onion, chopped
2	cloves garlic, minced
2	tablespoons dry sherry
½	cup plain low-fat yogurt
¼	teaspoon ground turmeric
¼	teaspoon paprika
¼	teaspoon ground cumin
⅛	teaspoon ground red pepper

Rinse split peas. In a large saucepan combine split peas, broth, bay leaf, and rosemary. Bring to boiling; reduce heat. Cover and simmer for 1 hour, stirring occasionally. Stir in celery, carrots, onion, and garlic. Return to boiling; reduce heat. Cover and simmer for 15 to 20 minutes more or till the vegetables are crisp-tender. Discard bay leaf. Stir in sherry.

Meanwhile, in a small bowl stir together the yogurt, turmeric, paprika, cumin, and red pepper.

To serve, ladle soup into soup bowls. Top each serving with the spiced yogurt mixture. Makes 4 servings.

Nutrition information per serving: 266 calories, 20 g protein, 40 g carbohydrate, 3 g fat (1 g saturated), 2 mg cholesterol, 852 mg sodium.

Chunky Potato-Pepper Soup

If you're serving this colorful soup to kids, reduce the ground red pepper to a dash for a milder flavor.

3   medium potatoes, cubed (2¼ cups)
2   cups vegetable or chicken broth
1   small green sweet pepper, chopped
1   small red sweet pepper, chopped
1   small yellow sweet pepper, chopped
1   small onion, chopped
¼   cup margarine or butter
¼   cup all-purpose flour
¼   teaspoon salt
¼   teaspoon black pepper
⅛   teaspoon ground red pepper
3   cups milk

In a medium saucepan combine potatoes and vegetable or chicken broth. Bring to boiling; reduce heat. Cover and simmer about 10 minutes or till the potatoes are tender. Do not drain.

Meanwhile, in a large saucepan cook the green pepper, red sweet pepper, yellow pepper, and onion in margarine or butter till tender. Stir in flour, salt, black pepper, and ground red pepper. Add milk all at once.

Cook and stir over medium heat till thickened and bubbly. Cook and stir for 1 minute more. Stir in undrained potatoes. Heat through. Makes 4 servings.

Nutrition information per serving: 344 calories, 12 g protein, 39 g carbohydrate, 16 g fat (5 g saturated), 14 mg cholesterol, 752 mg sodium.

Broth Options

Many of the recipes in this book call for vegetable broth, chicken broth, or beef broth. If you're fresh out of canned broth, you can use bouillon granules or cubes as an easy substitute. Just remember that 1 cup of canned broth is equivalent to 1 teaspoon of granules or 1 cup dissolved in 1 cup water. Look for canned broth and bouillon granules or cubes with the soups at your supermarket.

Pasta-Bean Soup with Fresh Herbs

Fresh basil and thyme take all the credit for the terrific taste of this soup. Do yourself a favor and use only fresh herbs.

2   cups sliced fresh mushrooms
1   medium onion, chopped
2   cloves garlic, minced
1   tablespoon margarine or butter
2   14½-ounce cans vegetable, chicken,
      or beef broth
½   cup packaged dried small pasta
      shells
1   15-ounce can garbanzo beans, rinsed
      and drained
1   14½-ounce can tomatoes, cut up
¼   cup snipped fresh basil
1   tablespoon snipped fresh thyme
      Fresh basil sprigs (optional)

In a large saucepan or Dutch oven cook the mushrooms, onion, and garlic in margarine or butter till tender. Add vegetable, chicken, or beef broth. Bring to boiling. Stir in the pasta. Return to boiling. Cook for 10 to 12 minutes or till pasta is tender but still firm. Stir in the garbanzo beans and undrained tomatoes. Heat through.

Just before serving, stir in snipped fresh basil and thyme. To serve, ladle soup into soup bowls. If desired, garnish with fresh basil sprigs. Makes 4 servings.

Nutrition information per serving: 213 calories, 9 g protein, 38 g carbohydrate, 6 g fat (1 g saturated), 0 mg cholesterol, 1,494 mg sodium.

Cheesy Vegetable Lasagna

If you like, substitute 1 cup chopped fresh mushrooms for the dried mushrooms. Simply cook the fresh mushrooms with the carrots, onion, and green pepper and use water instead of the dried mushroom liquid.

8 ounces packaged dried lasagna noodles (9 noodles)
1 cup boiling water
½ cup dried porcini or shiitake mushrooms (½ ounce)
2 medium carrots, chopped
1 large onion, chopped
1 large green sweet pepper, chopped
4 cloves garlic, minced
2 tablespoons margarine or butter
4 cups chopped broccoli (flowerets and stems)
1 15-ounce container ricotta cheese
1 cup shredded mozzarella cheese (4 ounces)
½ cup grated Parmesan or Romano cheese
2 eggs
¼ cup snipped parsley
½ teaspoon dried thyme, crushed
½ teaspoon dried marjoram, crushed
¼ teaspoon black pepper
1 30-ounce jar meatless spaghetti sauce
¼ cup grated Parmesan or Romano cheese

Cook lasagna noodles according to package directions. Drain. Meanwhile, in a medium bowl pour the boiling water over dried mushrooms. Let stand for 20 minutes. Drain and squeeze mushrooms, reserving ½ cup liquid. Remove and discard mushroom stems. Coarsely chop mushrooms. Set aside.

In a large skillet cook carrots, onion, green pepper, and garlic in margarine or butter till tender. Add broccoli and reserved mushroom liquid. Bring to boiling; reduce heat. Cover and simmer about 5 minutes or till the broccoli is just crisp-tender. Stir in the chopped mushrooms. Set aside.

In a medium bowl stir together the ricotta cheese, mozzarella cheese, ½ cup Parmesan or Romano cheese, eggs, parsley, thyme, marjoram, and black pepper.

To assemble, spread ½ cup of the spaghetti sauce in a 3-quart rectangular baking dish. Arrange 3 lasagna noodles over sauce. Top with half of the cheese mixture, half of the vegetable mixture, and 1 cup of the spaghetti sauce. Repeat layers, ending with noodles. Spoon the remaining spaghetti sauce over the top. Sprinkle with ¼ cup Parmesan or Romano cheese.

Cover and bake in a 375° oven for 20 minutes. Uncover and bake about 10 minutes more or till heated through. Makes 8 servings.

Nutrition information per serving: 485 calories, 30 g protein, 54 g carbohydrate, 20 g fat (8 g saturated), 86 mg cholesterol, 979 mg sodium.

Fresh Tomato Pizza with Pesto

For best results, make this recipe when ripe, juicy summer tomatoes are at their peak.

½ cup pesto
1 12-inch Italian bread shell (Boboli)
3 medium ripe tomatoes, thinly sliced
1 2¼-ounce can sliced pitted ripe olives, drained (scant ⅔ cup)
  Freshly ground pepper
2 cups shredded Monterey Jack or mozzarella cheese (8 ounces)

Spread pesto evenly over bread shell. Place on large pizza pan or baking sheet. Top with tomato slices. Sprinkle with olives and pepper. Top with Monterey Jack or mozzarella cheese.

Bake in a 425° oven for 10 to 15 minutes or till cheese is melted and tomatoes are warm. Cut into wedges. Makes 4 servings.

Nutrition information per serving: 776 calories, 32 g protein, 60 g carbohydrate, 48 g fat (11 g saturated), 60 mg cholesterol, 1,265 mg sodium.

Double Corn Tortilla Casserole

The double dose of corn comes from corn tortillas and whole kernel corn. Serve this tangy home-style dish with your favorite salsa or picante sauce.

8 6-inch corn tortillas
1½ cups shredded Monterey Jack cheese (6 ounces)
1 cup frozen whole kernel corn
4 green onions, sliced
2 eggs
1 cup buttermilk
1 4-ounce can diced green chili peppers

Grease a 2-quart square baking dish. Tear tortillas into bite-size pieces. Arrange half of the tortillas in prepared baking dish. Top with half of the cheese, half of the corn, and half of the green onions. Layer with the remaining tortillas, cheese, corn, and green onions.

In a medium mixing bowl stir together the eggs, buttermilk, and undrained chili peppers. Gently pour over tortilla mixture. Bake in a 325° oven about 30 minutes or till a knife inserted near the center comes out clean. Serve warm. Makes 4 servings.

Nutrition information per serving: 388 calories, 21 g protein, 37 g carbohydrate, 18 g fat (9 g saturated), 146 mg cholesterol, 564 mg sodium.

Fresh Tomato Pizza with Pesto

Cottage Cheese Puff

This airy baked casserole resembles a soufflé, but without all the fuss.

2　cups cottage cheese
¾　cup soft whole wheat bread crumbs
　　(about 1 slice bread)
½　cup all-purpose flour
⅓　cup snipped parsley
⅓　cup finely chopped green onions
2　tablespoons margarine or butter,
　　melted
¼　teaspoon salt
4　eggs
1　tablespoon snipped parsley

In a medium mixing bowl combine cottage cheese, bread crumbs, flour, ⅓ cup parsley, green onions, margarine or butter, and salt. Set aside.

In a large mixing bowl beat eggs with an electric mixer on high speed about 5 minutes or till thick and lemon colored. Gradually pour the cottage cheese mixture over the beaten eggs, folding to combine.

Pour the egg mixture into an ungreased 5- or 6-cup soufflé dish or casserole. Bake in a 350° oven about 1 hour or till a knife inserted near the center comes out clean. Sprinkle with 1 tablespoon parsley. Serve immediately. Makes 6 servings.

Nutrition information per serving: 205 calories, 15 g protein, 12 g carbohydrate, 11 g fat (4 g saturated), 152 mg cholesterol, 490 mg sodium.

Miniature Mexican Frittatas

These spunky little egg casseroles are baked in muffin cups and served with salsa. They make great breakfast or brunch fare.

1   10-ounce package frozen chopped
      spinach, thawed and well drained
1   cup cottage cheese, drained
½   cup grated Parmesan cheese
½   cup shredded cheddar cheese
      (2 ounces)
4   eggs
¼   cup milk
1   teaspoon ground cumin
¼   teaspoon pepper
2   tablespoons snipped cilantro or
      parsley
    Salsa, warmed
    Dairy sour cream (optional)

Lightly grease twelve 2½-inch muffin cups. Set aside. In a medium mixing bowl combine the spinach, cottage cheese, Parmesan cheese, and cheddar cheese. In another medium mixing bowl stir together the eggs, milk, cumin, and pepper. Stir into spinach mixture. Stir in the cilantro or parsley.

Spoon mixture into prepared muffin cups. Bake in a 375° oven for 20 to 25 minutes or till eggs are set. Let stand for 5 minutes. Remove from muffin cups. Serve with salsa and, if desired, sour cream. Serves 4.

Nutrition information per serving: 274 calories, 26 g protein, 9 g carbohydrate, 15 g fat (8 g saturated), 244 mg cholesterol, 738 mg sodium.

South-of-the-Border Pie

Beans, rice, eggs, and cheese provide the protein while chili powder and cumin provide the kick. Serve this with a simple tossed salad.

1 medium onion, chopped
2 cloves garlic, minced
1 tablespoon olive oil or cooking oil
1 to 2 teaspoons chili powder
1 teaspoon ground cumin
¼ teaspoon salt
1 15-ounce can red kidney beans,
    rinsed and drained
1½ cups cooked brown rice
1 cup shredded cheddar cheese
    (4 ounces)
¾ cup milk
2 slightly beaten eggs
    Green sweet pepper strips (optional)
    Salsa (optional)

Lightly grease a 10-inch quiche dish or pie plate. Set aside. In a large saucepan cook onion and garlic in hot oil till tender. Stir in chili powder, cumin, and salt. Cook and stir for 1 minute more. Cool. Stir in beans, cooked brown rice, cheese, milk, and eggs.

Spoon the bean mixture into the prepared baking dish. Bake in a 350° oven about 25 minutes or till the center is set. Let stand for 10 minutes. If desired, sprinkle the pie with green pepper strips and serve with salsa. Makes 6 servings.

Nutrition information per serving: 254 calories, 14 g protein, 26 g carbohydrate, 12 g fat (5 g saturated), 93 mg cholesterol, 366 mg sodium.

Sodium Sense for Beans

Using canned beans in recipes can save you time, but they also can contribute sodium to your diet. A simple solution to this salty situation is to rinse the beans in a colander under running water and let them drain. You'll still have great tasting beans without the salty liquid that comes with them.

Savory Shepherd's Pie

In a hurry? Substitute packaged instant mashed potatoes (enough for 4 servings) for the 3 small potatoes and stir the garlic mixture into the prepared instant potatoes.

3 small potatoes (12 ounces)
2 cloves garlic, minced
½ teaspoon dried basil, crushed
2 tablespoons margarine or butter
¼ teaspoon salt
2 to 4 tablespoons milk
1 medium onion, chopped
1 medium carrot, sliced
1 tablespoon cooking oil
1 15-ounce can kidney beans, rinsed
     and drained
1 14½-ounce can tomatoes, drained
     and cut up
1 10-ounce package frozen mixed
     vegetables or whole kernel corn
1 8-ounce can tomato sauce
1 teaspoon Worcestershire sauce
½ teaspoon sugar
1 cup shredded cheddar cheese
     (4 ounces)
   Paprika (optional)

Peel and quarter potatoes. In a covered large saucepan cook potatoes in a small amount of boiling, lightly salted water for 20 to 25 minutes or till tender. Drain.

Mash with a potato masher or beat with an electric mixer on low speed. In a small saucepan cook garlic and basil in margarine or butter for 15 seconds. Add to mashed potatoes along with salt. Gradually beat in enough of the milk to make light and fluffy. Set aside.

For filling, in a medium saucepan cook the onion and carrot in hot oil till onion is tender. Stir in kidney beans, tomatoes, frozen vegetables, tomato sauce, Worcestershire sauce, and sugar. Heat till bubbly.

Transfer vegetable mixture to an ungreased 8x8x2-inch baking pan. Drop mashed potatoes in 4 mounds over vegetable mixture. Sprinkle with cheddar cheese and, if desired, paprika.

Bake in a 375° oven for 25 to 30 minutes or till heated through and cheese starts to brown. Makes 4 servings.

Nutrition information per serving: 456 calories, 20 g protein, 60 g carbohydrate, 19 g fat (8 g saturated), 31 mg cholesterol, 1,130 mg sodium.

Two-Bean Tamale Pie

This mildly-seasoned kidney and pinto bean casserole is topped with a crusty corn bread hat. Serve it with your family's favorite salsa.

1   medium green sweet pepper, chopped
1   small onion, chopped
2   cloves garlic, minced
1   tablespoon cooking oil
1   15-ounce can kidney beans, rinsed, drained, and slightly mashed
1   15-ounce can pinto beans, rinsed, drained, and slightly mashed
1   6-ounce can (⅔ cup) vegetable juice
¼   cup snipped cilantro or parsley
1   teaspoon chili powder
1   teaspoon ground cumin
½   cup yellow cornmeal
½   cup whole wheat flour
1   teaspoon baking soda
¼   teaspoon salt
1   egg
½   cup buttermilk
1   4-ounce can diced green chili peppers
2   tablespoons cooking oil
½   cup shredded cheddar cheese (2 ounces)
    Sliced fresh chili peppers (optional)
    Cilantro sprigs (optional)

Grease a 10-inch quiche dish or a 2-quart square baking dish. Set aside. In a large skillet cook green pepper, onion, and garlic in 1 tablespoon hot oil till tender. Stir in the kidney beans, pinto beans, vegetable juice, snipped cilantro or parsley, chili powder, and cumin. Heat till bubbly. Spoon the bean mixture into prepared baking dish.

In a medium bowl stir together the cornmeal, flour, baking soda, and salt. Combine egg, buttermilk, undrained canned chili peppers, and 2 tablespoons oil. Add to cornmeal mixture, stirring just till combined. Fold in cheese. Spread cornmeal mixture evenly over bean mixture. Bake in a 400° oven about 20 minutes or till golden brown. If desired, garnish with fresh chili peppers and cilantro sprigs. Makes 6 servings.

Nutrition information per serving: 330 calories, 16 g protein, 45 g carbohydrate, 12 g fat (3 g saturated), 46 mg cholesterol, 856 mg sodium.

Southern Grits Casserole with Red Pepper Relish

To make a roasted pepper relish, substitute one 12-ounce jar roasted red sweet peppers for the fresh sweet peppers. Drain and chop the roasted peppers and stir into the cooked onion mixture.

4	cups water
1	cup quick-cooking grits
4	slightly beaten eggs
2	cups shredded cheddar cheese (8 ounces)
½	cup milk
¼	cup sliced green onions
1	to 2 jalapeño peppers, seeded (if desired) and chopped
½	teaspoon garlic salt
¼	teaspoon white pepper
	Sliced green onions (optional)
2	medium red sweet peppers, chopped (2 cups)
1	small red onion, chopped (½ cup)
2	cloves garlic, minced
1	tablespoon margarine or butter
⅓	cup snipped parsley
1	tablespoon white wine vinegar

In a large saucepan bring water to boiling. Slowly stir in grits. Gradually stir about 1 cup of the hot mixture into the eggs. Return to saucepan. Remove from heat.

Stir the shredded cheese, milk, ¼ cup green onions, jalapeño peppers, garlic salt, and white pepper into the grits mixture.

Spoon the grits mixture into an ungreased 2-quart casserole. Bake in a 350° oven for 45 to 50 minutes or till a knife inserted near the center comes out clean If desired, sprinkle with additional green onions.

Meanwhile, for relish, in a medium saucepan cook the red sweet peppers, red onion, and garlic in margarine or butter just till peppers are tender. Remove from heat. Stir in parsley and vinegar.

Let stand at room temperature at least 30 minutes. Serve the relish with grits. Makes 4 servings.

Nutrition information per serving: 403 calories, 23 g protein, 16 g carbohydrate, 27 g fat (14 g saturated), 275 mg cholesterol, 731 mg sodium.

Spaghetti Squash Italiano

Save time by cooking spaghetti squash in your microwave oven. Prick whole squash with a sharp knife. Place squash in a microwave-safe baking dish. Microwave, uncovered, on 100% power (high) for 15 to 20 minutes or till tender. Let stand for 5 minutes. Halve squash lengthwise and remove seeds.

2 small spaghetti squash (1¼ to 1½ pounds)
4 ounces mozzarella cheese, cut into small cubes (1 cup)
3 medium tomatoes, seeded and chopped (2 cups)
4 green onions, sliced
½ cup pine nuts or coarsely chopped walnuts, toasted
¼ cup snipped fresh basil or parsley
1 tablespoon olive oil or cooking oil
2 cloves garlic, minced
2 tablespoons grated Parmesan cheese

Halve the squash lengthwise and remove the seeds. Prick skin all over with a sharp knife. Place halves, cut sides down, in a 3-quart rectangular baking dish. Cover and bake in a 350° oven for 60 to 70 minutes or till squash is tender.

Using a fork, separate the squash pulp into strands, leaving strands in shells. Sprinkle one-fourth of the mozzarella cheese in each shell; toss lightly. Push the squash mixture up the sides of the shells.

Meanwhile, for filling, in a medium mixing bowl combine tomatoes, green onions, nuts, basil or parsley, oil, and garlic. Spoon the filling into squash shells. Sprinkle with Parmesan cheese.

Return to baking dish. Bake about 20 minutes more or till filling is heated through. Makes 4 servings.

Nutrition information per serving: 304 calories, 15 g protein, 23 g carbohydrate, 20 g fat (6 g saturated), 18 mg cholesterol, 237 mg sodium.

Crispy Eggplant with Tomato-Feta Cheese Sauce

For a mild cheese flavor, sprinkle feta cheese over the spaghetti sauce. For a more robust cheese flavor, use blue cheese.

1 medium eggplant (about 1 pound), peeled and thinly sliced
Salt
2 slightly beaten eggs
2 tablespoons milk
½ cup grated Parmesan cheese
½ cup toasted wheat germ
1 teaspoon dried basil, crushed
¼ teaspoon black pepper
2 cups meatless spaghetti sauce
¼ to ½ teaspoon ground red pepper
1 cup crumbled feta or blue cheese
Snipped fresh basil (optional)

Place eggplant slices on a baking sheet. Sprinkle lightly with salt. Let stand for 10 minutes. Pat eggplant dry with paper towels.

Grease a baking sheet. Set aside. In a shallow bowl combine the eggs and milk. In another shallow bowl stir together the Parmesan cheese, wheat germ, dried basil, and black pepper.

Dip the eggplant slices in egg mixture, then into wheat germ mixture, turning to coat both sides. Place the coated slices in a single layer on prepared baking sheet.

Bake in a 400° oven for 15 to 20 minutes or till the eggplant is crisp on outside and tender on inside.

Meanwhile, for sauce, in a medium saucepan combine the spaghetti sauce and ground red pepper. Cook over medium heat till heated through.

To serve, divide the eggplant slices among dinner plates. Spoon the sauce over eggplant. Sprinkle with feta or blue cheese and, if desired, snipped fresh basil. Makes 4 servings.

Nutrition information per serving: 388 calories, 20 g protein, 35 g carbohydrate, 20 g fat (9 g saturated), 142 mg cholesterol, 1,471 mg sodium.

Golden Fettuccine Soufflé

Baby food carrots help make this soufflé golden and save you time in the kitchen. But if you prefer to use fresh carrots, cook 2 cups chopped or sliced carrots in a small amount of boiling, lightly salted water about 20 minutes or till tender. Drain well. Purée in a food processor or blender.

4   ounces packaged dried fettuccine or linguine, broken into 1-inch pieces (1⅓ cups)
¼   cup chopped onion
1   clove garlic, minced
3   tablespoons margarine or butter
¼   cup all-purpose flour
2   teaspoons snipped fresh dill or ½ teaspoon dried dillweed
½   teaspoon salt
¼   teaspoon pepper
1   cup milk
3   4-ounce jars puréed baby food carrots
2   egg yolks
4   egg whites

Cook pasta according to package directions. Drain. Meanwhile, in a medium saucepan cook onion and garlic in margarine or butter till tender.

Stir in the flour, fresh dill or dried dillweed, salt, and pepper. Add milk all at once. Cook and stir over medium heat till thickened and bubbly. Remove from heat. Stir in baby food carrots and cooked pasta.

In a medium mixing bowl beat egg yolks with a fork till combined. Gradually add carrot mixture, stirring constantly. Set aside.

In a large bowl beat egg whites till stiff peaks form (tips stand straight). Gently fold about 1 cup of the egg whites into the carrot mixture. Gradually pour carrot mixture over remaining egg whites, folding to combine. Pour into an ungreased 1½-quart soufflé dish or a 2-quart square baking dish.

Bake in a 350° oven for 35 to 40 minutes or till a knife inserted near the center comes out clean. Serve immediately. Makes 4 servings.

Nutrition information per serving: 310 calories, 12 g protein, 36 g carbohydrate, 13 g fat (3 g saturated), 111 mg cholesterol, 480 mg sodium.

Four Bean Enchiladas

Using canned beans makes this dish a snap to prepare. We chose kidney, garbanzo, pinto, and navy or great northern beans but you can use any combination of beans that you like.

16 6-inch corn tortillas
 1 15-ounce can red kidney beans,
     rinsed and drained
 1 15-ounce can garbanzo beans, rinsed
     and drained
 1 15-ounce can pinto beans, rinsed
     and drained
 1 15-ounce can navy or great northern
     beans, rinsed and drained
 1 11-ounce can condensed cheddar
     cheese or nacho cheese soup
 1 10-ounce can enchilada sauce
 1 8-ounce can tomato sauce
1½ cups shredded Monterey Jack or
     cheddar cheese (6 ounces)
     Sliced pitted ripe olives (optional)
     Green sweet pepper strips (optional)

Wrap tortillas in foil and bake in a 350° oven about 10 minutes or till warm.

For filling, in a large mixing bowl combine beans and cheese soup. Spoon about ⅓ cup filling onto one end of each tortilla. Starting from the end with the filling, roll up each tortilla.

Arrange tortillas, seam sides down, in 2 ungreased 2-quart rectangular baking dishes or 8 individual au gratin dishes.

In a medium mixing bowl stir together the enchilada sauce and tomato sauce. Pour over tortillas.

Cover and bake in the 350° oven about 30 minutes for baking dishes (about 20 minutes for au gratin dishes) or till heated through. Sprinkle with shredded cheese.

Bake, uncovered, about 5 minutes more or till cheese is melted. If desired, sprinkle with ripe olives and green pepper strips. Makes 8 servings.

Nutrition information per serving: 491 calories, 25 g protein, 71 g carbohydrate, 14 g fat (7 g saturated), 29 mg cholesterol, 1,599 mg sodium.

Tofu and Cheese-Stuffed Shells

No one will ever know that these giant pasta shells contain tofu…unless you tell.

12 packaged dried jumbo pasta shells
¼ cup shredded carrot
1 green onion, sliced
8 ounces tofu (fresh bean curd), drained
½ cup ricotta cheese
½ cup shredded cheddar cheese
½ cup shredded mozzarella cheese
1 egg white
¼ teaspoon salt
¼ teaspoon pepper
1 14½-ounce can tomatoes, cut up
½ of a 6-ounce can (⅓ cup) tomato paste
1 teaspoon dried basil, crushed
1 teaspoon dried oregano, crushed
½ teaspoon sugar
¼ teaspoon garlic powder
¼ teaspoon fennel seed, crushed (optional)
   Grated Parmesan cheese (optional)

Cook pasta according to package directions. Drain pasta; rinse with cold water. Drain again.

Meanwhile, in a small saucepan cook carrot and green onion in a small amount of water till tender. Drain.

For filling, in a medium mixing bowl mash tofu with a fork. Stir in carrot mixture, ricotta cheese, cheddar cheese, ¼ cup of the mozzarella cheese, egg white, salt, and pepper. Set aside.

For sauce, in a medium saucepan combine undrained tomatoes, tomato paste, basil, oregano, sugar, garlic powder, and, if desired, fennel seed. Bring to boiling; reduce heat. Simmer, uncovered, for 10 minutes.

To assemble, stuff each pasta shell with about 1 rounded tablespoon filling. Place in an ungreased 2-quart square baking dish. Pour sauce over shells.

Cover and bake in a 350° oven about 25 minutes or till heated through. Sprinkle with the remaining mozzarella cheese. If desired, serve with Parmesan cheese. Makes 4 servings.

Nutrition information per serving: 318 calories, 21 g protein, 32 g carbohydrate, 13 g fat (6 g saturated), 32 mg cholesterol, 558 mg sodium.

Tossed Meatless Salad Nicoise

Dress up this easy salad with small yellow pear tomatoes when they are in season.

2 medium potatoes, sliced ¼ inch
   thick
1 9-ounce package frozen cut green
   beans
1 cup cherry tomatoes, halved
1 small yellow or green sweet pepper,
   cut into strips
½ cup Greek olives or pitted ripe olives
¾ cup Italian salad dressing
4 cups torn romaine lettuce
4 hard-cooked eggs, sliced

In a covered medium saucepan cook the potatoes in boiling, lightly salted water for 5 minutes. Break up frozen beans; add to potatoes in saucepan. Return to boiling; reduce heat. Cover and simmer for 4 to 6 minutes more or till potatoes are tender and green beans are just crisp-tender. Drain and cool slightly.

In a large salad bowl combine the potato mixture, cherry tomatoes, sweet pepper, and olives. Pour salad dressing over mixture. Toss gently to coat. Cover and chill for 2 to 3 hours.

To serve, line dinner plates with romaine. Top with vegetable mixture and egg slices. Makes 4 servings.

Nutrition information per serving: 410 calories, 11 g protein, 29 g carbohydrate, 30 g fat (5 g saturated), 213 mg cholesterol, 507 mg sodium.

Layered Taco Salad

For a spicier version of this pretty tiered salad, use Monterey Jack cheese with jalapeño peppers.

1	15-ounce can black beans, rinsed and drained
4	cups shredded iceberg lettuce
1	medium tomato, seeded and chopped (⅔ cup)
1½	cups shredded cheddar or Monterey Jack cheese (6 ounces)
¼	cup sliced pitted ripe olives
¼	cup sliced green onions
1	6-ounce carton frozen avocado dip, thawed
½	cup dairy sour cream
1	4-ounce can diced green chili peppers, drained
1	tablespoon milk
1	clove garlic, minced
½	teaspoon chili powder
	Chopped tomato (optional)
2	cups coarsely crushed tortilla chips

In a 2½-quart glass salad bowl layer the black beans, shredded lettuce, ⅔ cup chopped tomato, shredded cheese, ripe olives, and green onions.

For dressing, in a medium bowl stir together avocado dip, sour cream, chili peppers, milk, garlic, and chili powder. Spread over the top of the salad. If desired, sprinkle with additional chopped tomato. Cover the surface with plastic wrap and chill for 2 to 24 hours.

Before serving, toss salad together. Serve over crushed tortilla chips. Makes 4 servings.

Nutrition information per serving: 561 calories, 24 g protein, 37 g carbohydrate, 40 g fat (14 g saturated), 58 mg cholesterol, 1,277 mg sodium.

Grilled Vegetable Salad with Garlic Dressing

Vegetables, sweet and smoky from the grill, give pasta and cheese a jolt of flavor and color. By doing the grilling ahead, and storing the savory dressing in the refrigerator, this maximum-impact dish is done in the time it takes to simmer pasta. (Also pictured on the cover.)

2   red and/or yellow sweet peppers
2   Japanese eggplants, halved
      lengthwise
2   medium zucchini or yellow summer
      squash, halved lengthwise, or
      8 to 10 yellow sunburst or
      pattypan squash*
1   tablespoon olive oil
2   cups packaged dried rigatoni or
      mostaccioli
      Roasted Garlic Dressing
¾   cup cubed fontina cheese (3 ounces)
1   to 2 tablespoons snipped Italian
      flat-leaf or curly parsley
      Italian flat-leaf parsley sprigs
      (optional)

Halve sweet peppers lengthwise; remove and discard stems, seeds, and membranes. Brush sweet peppers, eggplants, and squash with olive oil.

Grill vegetables on an uncovered grill directly over medium-hot coals for 8 to 12 minutes or till the vegetables are tender, turning occasionally. Remove vegetables from grill; cool slightly. Cut vegetables into 1-inch pieces.

Meanwhile, cook the pasta according to package directions. Drain pasta; rinse with cold water. Drain again. In a large bowl combine the pasta and grilled vegetables. Pour Roasted Garlic Dressing over pasta mixture. Toss gently to coat. Stir in fontina cheese. Sprinkle with snipped parsley. If desired, garnish with parsley sprigs. Makes 4 servings.

Roasted Garlic Dressing: In a screw-top jar combine 3 tablespoons *balsamic vinegar* or *red wine vinegar,* 2 tablespoons *olive oil,* 1 tablespoon *water,* 1 teaspoon bottled *roasted minced garlic,* ¼ teaspoon *salt,* and ¼ teaspoon *black pepper.* Cover and shake well.

*Note: If using sunburst or pattypan squash, cook the squash in a small amount of boiling water for 3 minutes before grilling.

Nutrition information per serving: 369 calories, 12 g protein, 40 g carbohydrate, 19 g fat (6 g saturated), 61 mg cholesterol, 317 mg sodium.

Cheese and Veggie Sandwiches

If you're watching your sodium intake, you can reduce the salt in cottage cheese by placing it in a colander and rinsing under cold water.

1½ cups cottage cheese, drained
¼ cup shredded carrot
¼ cup chopped celery or green sweet
    pepper
½ teaspoon finely snipped fresh chives
¼ cup plain low-fat yogurt
8 small slices whole grain bread
2 tablespoons horseradish mustard
    Spinach or lettuce leaves
4 tomato slices

In a medium bowl combine the cottage cheese, carrot, celery or green pepper, and chives. Stir in the yogurt.

Spread the bread slices with horseradish mustard. Place the spinach or lettuce leaves on half of the bread slices. Top with the cottage cheese mixture, tomato slices, and the remaining bread slices. Makes 4 servings.

Nutrition information per serving: 232 calories, 16 g protein, 29 g carbohydrate, 7 g fat (3 g saturated), 13 mg cholesterol, 722 mg sodium.

Sautéed Onion & Tomato Sandwiches

When laps double as the dining table, the best TV dinner is something easy and out-of-hand. This hearty whole-grain sandwich serves perfectly. Pass around beer, brownies, and your biggest napkins.

2   medium onions, sliced
1   teaspoon olive oil
8   slices hearty whole grain bread
       (toasted, if desired)
     Honey mustard
4   lettuce leaves, shredded
3   small red and/or yellow tomatoes,
       thinly sliced
     Small fresh basil leaves
4   ounces spreadable Brie cheese or
       ½ of an 8-ounce tub cream cheese

In a large skillet cook the onion slices in hot olive oil over medium-high heat for 5 to 7 minutes or till tender and just starting to brown. Remove from heat. Cool onions slightly.

To assemble, lightly spread half of the bread slices with honey mustard. Top with lettuce, onion slices, and tomato slices. Sprinkle with basil.

Spread the remaining bread slices with Brie or cream cheese. Place on top of sandwiches. Makes 4 servings.

Nutrition information per serving: 287 calories, 12 g protein, 35 g carbohydrate, 12 g fat (6 g saturated), 28 mg cholesterol, 490 mg sodium.

INDEX